# WALKING INTO

# THE BUISNESS

# WORLD

## The ultimate essentials in
## Starting your own business

# BOB RYAN

# TABLE OF CONTENT

# INTRODUCTION

A successful start-up is not built by one person alone, so surround yourself with subject matter experts and mentors you can lean on and learn from. Don't be afraid of failure; instead, learn from your mistakes and pivot your business model as needed. Test new ideas and acquire feedback so you can tweak your product to better meet customers' needs.

Although there are several start-up mistakes you'll want to avoid while building your business, occasional mistakes are inevitable. Don't be too hard on yourself during the process. One of the best things you can do is take what might first seem like bad news, learn from it and put it to good use. With that mentality, business success can be right around the corner.

# CHAPTER 1

## Things to Do Before Starting a Business

Starting a business can be stressful. It often feels like there are 1,000 things to work on all at the same time. There's no avoiding this reality for new small business owners. Still, with a little planning, it's possible to manage expectations and take actions with a sense of purpose toward building your business.

### 1. Do your research.

You want to make sure you understand the industry you'll be involved in so you can dominate. No matter how unique you might think your business idea is, you should be aware of competitors "Just because you have a brilliant idea does not mean other people haven't also had the same idea," said Wright. "If you can't offer something better and/or cheaper than your competitors, you might want to rethink starting a business in that area."

### 2. Determine your audience.

Spend time considering who your target demographic is. This audience will be the driving force in each decision you make. Understanding who needs your product or service can help fine-tune your offerings and ensure your marketing and sales strategies are reaching the right people. Part of this decision is understanding if you are a business-to-consumer (B2C) or business-to-business (B2B) enterprise. Within those parameters are multiple categories, including but certainly not limited to age, gender, income and profession. You can't earn a profit without your customers, so understand who they are and make them your priority. It is crucial to make sure you are delivering what your customer wants, not what you want

## 3. Have a strong mission.

Standing out is no easy feat, and no one magic formula guarantees results. However, knowing your business's purpose is central to guiding these decisions. By recognizing your business's strengths, differences, and purpose, you can make informed choices to expand your services and markets down the line in a way that is harmonious.

## 4. Choose a structure.

A key initial step to take when starting your business is choosing its legal structure. It will dictate the taxes, paperwork, liability of the owner and other legal aspects, as well as whether or not the company can have employees.

Additionally, you must acquire the proper local and state registration required to open your business.

This means the entrepreneur will need to create the articles of incorporation, obtain an employer identification number and apply for necessary licenses, which will vary by state and industry.

5. Map your finances.

Starting a business requires money that you likely won't have right away. This is why you need to seek out ways to acquire capital.

Most entrepreneurs start a business with a very limited amount of capital, which is a large hurdle to many. However, plenty of options are available to a budding business owner. The first and most common place to seek capital is with friends and family. If that is not enough, expand the search to angel investors and venture capitalists. Should these options not provide the amount needed, then apply for business loans through banks and small business associations?

6. Understand your tax burden.

There are multiple payments to make, and filing any of them late could result in severe consequences. You have to figure out how much your payroll will be to make your tax payments timely. The timing can vary depending on your payroll. You must also figure out other business taxes, such as city, county and state.

7. Understand the risk.

Of course, launching a new business venture will always involve a level of risk. Calculating, understanding and planning for risk is an important step to take before you start working on your business. This means assessing your industry's risks before developing a business plan.

Entrepreneurs should know their industry's risks before purchasing business insurance. For example, accountants will want to consider professional liability insurance if a client files a lawsuit, claiming a costly error on their tax return. Restaurant owners are more likely to need general liability for slip-and fall accidents and liquor liability insurance, which can pay for lawsuits.

8. Put together a business plan.

A business plan outlines the steps you need to take for a successful launch and continued growth. This document is important for establishing a focus for your business, attracting C-level professionals to work for you, and seeking and retaining capital. A business plan ensures you put your best foot forward with other professionals who are evaluating your company, so be sure to have this document on the back burner and ready when requested.

Take the time to put together the main components, including:

- Your mission statement
- A description of your business
- A list of your products or services
- An analysis of the current market and opportunity
- A list of decision-makers in the company, along with their bios
- Your financial plan so those who review can understand the opportunity

9. Time it right.

Timing is an important element of building a business. Sure, you want to start your business at a time when the economy is healthy and your prospective industry is expanding, but there's also a flow to decision-making that's important to be aware of.

I wish I understood how detrimental the role of time can be in building a business. If I could have had that mind-set from day one, I would probably have had fewer sleepless nights when I was going through tough times.

10. Look for a mentor or advisor.

Starting a business should not be an independent journey, no matter how tempting that sounds. Finding those who have made this journey before can help set you up for success. Network with other professionals in your industry, attend industry-specific workshops and events, and reach out to thought leaders in your industry to learn their approach. Alternatively, you may want to consider hiring a coach who can give you pointed advice.

11. Bring in the professionals.

Entrepreneurs can't know everything about running their new venture. Tapping into seasoned professionals' experience can ensure you're starting on the right foot. It's especially important to have legal assistance to ensure you are protected and going about the process correctly.

We often assume that legal counsel is for when we get ourselves into trouble, but preventative and proactive legal preparation can be the best way to set your business on the path to long-term success. When you call on legal counsel after you've run into a problem, it's often too late or could critically impact your business in both the short and long term. Investing in their insight at the start of your business can pay a huge return later on by keeping you out of trouble before you even get into it.

# CHAPTER 2

## How to determine if you have a good business idea

Sometimes inspiration isn't the problem; the challenge is determining whether you have a good idea. Critiquing your idea and requesting feedback from as many people as possible is crucial.

1. Does your business idea solve a problem?

If there is a problem that affects you, your friends, family and co-workers, then the chances are high that it affects people you don't know as well.

2. Will people pay for it?

Whether you're focused on a creative new business idea or have an idea for an easy-to-start business, you'll need customers. Paying customers validate an idea and determine which ones have the greatest chance for success. An idea is just an idea until you have a paying customer attached to it.

3. What's your price point?

A great business ideas solve problems in a way that is less expensive than what the market will endure. Once you have determined that you are solving a legitimate problem in a scalable way, you need to determine not only the value that it delivers to the world but what people would pay for that value. Once you determine the price, then you can assess if your solution is business worthy or not. Pricing your offerings can be tricky. Low prices can scare away customers, while overpricing can limit sales. You need to set a price point that works for everyone while managing customers' perception.

4. Is there a sizable niche market for your business idea?

Without a large enough market, your idea may never get off the ground. You must determine if a niche market exists for your idea. You're better poised for success if your company improves upon what's already out there.

5. Are you passionate enough about your business idea?

Your business will likely consume all your time, so ensure you're passionate about it to make it successful. Your idea must be something you genuinely care about, not just something you've targeted because it seems like it could be lucrative.

Since starting a business requires an inordinate amount of time, energy and patience, ideally the idea will be one that you are passionate about as well as one that you have skills or experience in.

6. Have you tested your business idea?

You won't know if it's viable until you test your business idea on strangers who match the profile of your target customer. Test it not just with friends who will be too polite to tell the truth but with honest people who would make up your ideal target audience, and then listen to the feedback. If your target sample is saying your idea is fantastic and asking where can they get it, you know that you're onto something. But if they are less than enthusiastic, it's probably not as good an idea as you thought.

## 7. Are you open to advice?

If you're not open to changing or adapting your idea to fit what your customers want, your business idea might not be worth pursuing. Success happens when you are willing to listen and consider others' advice. Most good ideas take some tweaking to get to market. Being closed-minded is a business killer.

## 8. How will you market your business?

Many entrepreneurs think about the problems their business will solve but not how they intend to market their company to their target customers. Your small business marketing strategy can determine if your business idea is good.

If you have a solid go-to-market strategy and a decent product, you'll probably be successful. But if you have a great product without any idea how to reach potential customers, then it's going to be really tough to make it successful.

9. Are you being realistic about your goals?

As excited as you may be about a new business idea, staying grounded and realistic is essential. You shouldn't have a Field of Dreams mentality when starting your business. Just because you have a vision and decide to build it does not mean the rest will follow. While you may have an idea that is original, revolutionary or ahead of its time, there should be a real, solid market opportunity to ensure it is successful. Any new business case or new endeavour has to have a viable market that you believe you can sell now, not theoretically or on the premise that there is a future for this market.

# CHAPTER 3

## How to Choose a Business Name

## That's Right for Your Company

A company name is your introduction to customers. It's what consumers will refer to every time they have any interaction with your company. Company names leave lasting impressions. Catchy brand names can make the difference between a business hooking its audience or disappearing in a crowd.

When you're figuring out how to come up with a company name, think of its value proposition. In other words, how your company brings value and is better than your competition. Your company name can increase your value proposition and set the standard of what customers can expect.

It's more than just how to come up with a brand name, but also how that name holds up to various factors, including:

- How clear is the name? Does it sound like a business?

- Is it a memorable or catchy name?

- Is it simple and easy to spell?

- Will the name be long-lasting? Is it trendy but not too trendy that it'll feel outdated in five years?

- Does this name help search engine optimization (SEO) at all?

- Is it authentic to your business?

- Does the name fit your audience demographic?

- Will your name work in other languages?

## Naming Your Business

1. Define your brand:

If you haven't done extensive branding work for your company, now is the time. Figure out your brand identity, the personality, tone, and positioning for your business. Pin down your target market with research. Your brand identity is the best place to start when naming your business.

2. Determine your name's criteria:

Define what you want from your brand name. Going off your branding, determine a specific feeling you want your company name to capture. Write it down, so you have a particular goal in mind and for something to compare your ideas against later.  Also, pin down any other criteria that are important to you, such as uniqueness or simplicity. Don't limit your creativity. But knowing what you're aiming for will help you in the process and give you a way to see if the names you come up with meet your goal.

3.  Brainstorm:

Now it's time to get creative. Brainstorming can be done in many different ways, depending on what works best for your business. Maybe your team wants to have a loose meeting to exchange ideas, or you'd prefer a more structured approach to workshop your best ideas. Look at companies you admire or those in your category. Rounding up these relevant brand names can help get creative juices flowing.  See what your competitors in your niche are named. Not only will that help you head in another direction, but it can act as inspiration to be more creative than the competition. Visualizing your business name helps it become more realistic and lets you picture what it might look like in various scenarios.

Plan to do the brainstorming process a few times to get a lot of ideas. Don't be too critical during this stage. A bad idea can lead you down the path to your perfect brand name.

4. Ask for feedback:

Once you cast a wide net of name ideas, you can start to narrow your options down with help from an audience. That can be friends, families, employees, or customers. Consider doing some audience testing to see how your potential names come across. You might be missing some meanings or connotations you don't want to be associated with your brand.

# CHAPTER 4

## Mistakes to avoid when starting your business

### 1. being afraid to fail

The biggest mistake you can make is to be afraid of failure. Failure is key to your success, and jumping into your fear is very positive for your future business. How you pick up after failure and learn from your mistakes is the key to great success.

### 2. Not making a business plan

Too many businesses start without a basic plan, and if you fail to plan, you are essentially planning to fail. A start-up should map out a business plan, even if it is just one page. It should include how much it costs to operate, how much they anticipate selling, who would buy their product and why.

### 3. Being disorganized

Being organized is key. Running a small business is like being a circus ringmaster. It's normal to have dozens of things happening at once. So, I have a daily task list, things that I need to do, and I list them by their priority. It sounds simple, but it works and makes me far more productive.

## 4. Not defining your market and target audience

A common start-up mistake is not taking the time to understand the market or customers you're building for. For technical founders, writing code can seem easier than talking to customers, but there's no way to know if you're on the right track unless you're constantly getting feedback from current or prospective customers. It's important to recognize that building a great product often doesn't translate into a successful business.

## 5. Not filing for the proper legal structure

The biggest mistakes start-ups make are not registering their business, picking the right business entity or protecting their intellectual property. These three areas are crucial to a business starting right, where, if not done properly, will cost valuable time and money to correct.

## 6. Trying to do everything yourself

A big mistake entrepreneurs make is thinking they are all alone, and they try to operate independently without surrounding themselves with wise counsel. Don't try to run a new business by yourself. Find an on board trustworthy seasoned advisors to discuss your business ideas, strategy, challenges and progress. Wisdom and power exist in the multiplicity of counsel.

## 7. Partnering with the wrong investors

An important piece of advice that entrepreneurs should know before starting a business is that their investors are more than just financial backers. A company's first set of investors will make or break it. These individuals place their confidence in the business's potential without having a proof of concept presented to them. Once businesses have undergone their seed funding, then they'll interact with investors who look at the business's growth and sustainability.

## 8. Avoiding contracts

One of the biggest mistakes a business owner/entrepreneur can make when starting a business is the failure to implement contracts. No matter how good relationships may be, they can come to a screeching halt when systems and agreements are not put in place.

## 9. Hiring too soon

By far, the biggest mistake a start-up can make is hiring employees too soon, such as hiring full-timers when a part-timer might make more sense or hiring an employee when a subcontractor could have done the same job/function. It is very easy to run a small business with part-timers, subcontractors and the services of other professionals.

## 10. Underestimating capital requirements

Most entrepreneurs think they can get further with less. In an effort to minimize equity dilution, they forget to factor in unknowns, challenges or delays along the way. Start-up leaders tend to plan for the best-case scenario, but that almost never happens. Positivity has its place, however, when it comes to capital; it often results in having to go back to the well for a less-than-ideal raise.

## 11. Wasting money

Handling money incorrectly and being irresponsible with cash flow is a death sentence for start-ups with limited access to capital. I've made the mistake of hiring too many people instead of the right people and spending money to fill the top of the funnel without having a well-defined process to manage the bottom of the funnel. Putting good money to bad use and trying to be everything to everyone instead of being niche-focused is a sure-fire way to waste valuable time and money, which are the lifeblood to any start-up

## 12. Giving yourself the wrong salary

Paying yourself too little or too much is a mistake. It's often easier to determine the salary for a new hire than determining an owner or partner's pay. Consider paying yourself a percentage of revenue. Whatever you choose, make figuring out your pay and that of your partners a practice and foundation to healthy expectation of management.

## 13. Undervaluing your product or service

Don't price too high, but don't price too low just to gain market share. If you are good, price like it! Many entrepreneurs start with the best of intentions and give things away for free or do free things for charity, community or visibility. Be very careful with this because you don't want to be known as a source of freebies.

## 14. Launching too quickly

One of the biggest mistakes start-ups make is launching before they are ready. The saying 'Done is better than perfect' is the right advice; however, the 'done' needs to ensure it can handle new clients. Once you have launched into the public and you start getting clients, ensure your systems and processes are in place – such as payment terms and process, contracts, communications – whilst still being able to maintain your marketing strategy. The back-end processes need to be watertight before you start taking on clients; if they aren't, these are the cracks that will show and appear unprofessional.

## 15. Expanding too quickly

When you start to see success, it can be easy to assume that growth will continue and the best way to make the most out of it is to simply copy and paste your working formula. However, if you … expand your business too rapidly, it could have dire consequences. You may find your period of growth was only temporary and end up stuck with a bunch of new staff but no work and no funds to cover them. That's why it's important to take a slow and steady approach to expansion and never act on a spur of good results.

## 16. Not implementing a proper bookkeeping process

Many start-up founders begin without a bookkeeping process in place. Great bookkeeping habits help you make smarter business decisions, spot opportunities early on, and head off problems before they become unmanageable. Understanding your financials helps to keep a pulse on your business's financial health. Good bookkeeping practices also ensure you're on top of issues like tax and insurance payments that can get otherwise great businesses into trouble.

## 17. Not creating a marketing plan

If you have successfully validated the problem, market and idea for your start-up, then you need to have a plan for how you're going to get your first user, first 10 users, first 50 users and so on. That's where you need a detailed marketing strategy that encompasses the initial acquisition of users, the conversion of those users into paying customers, and making those customers so happy with your product that they help you get more users.

## 18. Hiring the wrong people

Different skill sets and backgrounds are needed for the different positions you'll want to fill. When you get started, make sure you have hardworking, all-around generalists who can do everything you need them to do. When you begin to grow, look at hiring those who are specialized for the roles that need a specialist. Don't hire a generalist when you need someone who is specialized, and don't hire a specialist when you could hire a generalist to do it.

## 19. Overpromising

Don't overstretch yourself in the pursuit of revenue. It is far better to tell a potential customer that you can take on their project next month, for example, rather than take on too much. Not only will this save you from failing to meet targets due to an increased workload, but it will also make you look like you're in high demand.

# CHAPTER 5

## Common Challenges Faced By Start-ups

Challenges are everywhere. Businesses in general and start-ups in particular are no exception to myriad of challenges that we face today.

1. Fierce Competition

The corporate world is quite fierce. There is always a competition going on between the giants. Competition poses one of the biggest challenges for the survival of start-up businesses. And if you have an online business start-up, the competition gets tougher.

The competitive environment keeps the start-ups on their toes, as there is no margin of error available. Both B2B and B2C organizations always tend to feel the heat of the fierce competition. In order to survive in this competitive business environment that covers both traditional and online businesses, the start-ups need to play aggressively, and punch above their weight to gain the much needed recognition amongst the clusters of ever challenging and expanding businesses.

## 2. Unrealistic Expectations

Success does not come alone. It brings expectations with it. Most of the times, these expectations seem realistic, But in the real sense of the word, are merely unrealistic. This same concept holds true for young start-ups.

Start-ups tend to face challenges when they set 'unrealistic expectations' following a booming success. Remember, success is short-lived and expectations never end. This is where start-ups need to translate what the real expectations are? Sustainability is the name of the game. And sustainability requires consistent efforts.

In order to succeed in a competitive business world, start-ups need to have high but controlled expectations, keeping view of the resources available, the extent of growth potential, and other market factors as well.

## 3. Hiring Suitable Candidates

One of the most important factors that define organizational culture within a start-up company is the synergy of the team. A team comprises of individuals with similar capabilities and identical focus. In order to develop a highly successful team culture, organizations in general and start-ups in particular need to hire suitable candidates.

There is a huge pool of aspiring individuals available. Selecting a suitable candidate that fits the job well enough is a peculiarly tricky task. It is one of the biggest challenges facing the start-up businesses in this digital age. When hiring a suitable candidate, organizations must remember one golden rule: Birds of a feather flock together.

4. Partnership Decision Making

Partnership is the essence of success. And this logic holds true for start-ups as well. In this ever-expanding and ever-changing digital era, where organizations need to battle hard for their survival, start-ups also find it difficult to find trustworthy partners. It's really a big challenge for start-ups today. And as far as tech start-ups are concerned, stakes in partnership are much higher for them.

Going into a partnership pays great dividends for the start-ups, but they need to consider a variety of factors before making any decision to collaborate with another company working in the same ecosystem. To reap out maximum benefits out of a partnership, start-up businesses should look for organizations that enjoy a sound presence within the market and a good reputation amongst the industry giants.

## 5. Financial Management

Money begets money. Remember the fact that when income increases, the expenditures also increase. There is no doubt about it. One of the biggest challenges that start-ups face today relates to financial management.

It is a fact that small start-ups rely heavily on financial backups from the so called investors. At times, when there is a cash influx, small firms, most importantly start-ups tend to find it really hard to properly manage their finances, and they bog down against the pressure.

In order to address this kind of situation, start-ups need to play a safe and cautious hand, by keeping all the cards close to their chests. Taking help from a reputed financial consultancy firm may really help out in managing financial crises facing today's start-up businesses.

## 6. Cyber Security

This is the digital age. And surviving the challenges in this age requires small start-ups – especially the ones operating online – to be super agile to counter the so called online security threats. Hackers are everywhere, and they are going to take advantage of any loophole within the systems installed within a start-up firm.

The rate of cybercrimes has increased dramatically during the past couple of years. The percentage is going to increase in the coming years as well. Start-ups that are active online do face online security threats. Be it unauthorized access to start-up's sensitive information, employee records, bank accounts' information, or any other related information that is deemed important for the survival of a tech start-up, they are at risk.

In order to safeguard the all-important online data, start-ups need to have robust and military-grade security systems in place. A virtual private network (VPN) connection serves the purpose of protecting a start-up's information, and employee records, by offering the much needed encryption and data security to the start-up's employees, thereby restricting unauthorized access to organizational data over the web.

## 7. Winning Trust of Customers

Customer is the king. And that's absolutely right. Winning a customer's trust is one of the most important challenges that businesses in general and start-ups in particular face today. With a highly satisfied and loyal customer base, start-ups can scale and make progress towards excellence.

Customers are the real force behind a start-up's success. Their word-of-mouth power and their presence on social media can give tech start-ups an edge against all the traditional businesses.

To win customers' trust and loyalty, start-ups need to work aggressively to implement a customer-centric working philosophy, so as to enable them to succeed in their pursuit of attaining the height sustainable growth and progress they desire to achieve in this tech-savvy and challenging business world.

# CHAPTER 6

## Avoiding business failure

The fear of failure is one of the most common reasons why people decide not to start their own business. Hauling yourself out of your comfort zone and throwing yourself into the unknown takes a certain amount of courage and self-assurance. Leaving a cosy, secure job to try and turn your business idea into reality is definitely a risk, but if you follow sound advice you're more likely to succeed.

### 1. DIY market research

The only way to know for sure is to carry out market research. That in itself may sound like a big, expensive project, but it doesn't need to be. Speak to friends and family, search around for competing ideas online or create a quick survey to get feedback on your product and insight into your market.

### 2. Share your ideas

Lots of people keep their killer business idea to themselves, worried that others will run off with their brainwave if they share it, but this is unfounded. Having a great idea is all very well and good, but having the determination and dedication to follow it through and build it into a success is far more important. Share your idea, get feedback and use it to help shape your plans.

### 3. Set realistic goals

One of the things that tends to intimidate people when they're starting out is the sheer amount to do. It's very easy to get caught up with the small details, such as creating the perfect logo, or constantly refining the extensive business plan. But what you need to do is set your sights on growth and customer acquisition. The other stuff can wait. Set your sights on simple objectives that you can work towards now and throw all your energy into achieving those.

### 4. Be patient with success

Success can take time, and anyone who thinks they're going to be a hit overnight is pretty likely to end up disappointed. Two thirds of the people we surveyed said that growing their customer base is the single biggest difficulty their business face. We all go through it, and a clear lesson for any entrepreneur is that you're very likely to encounter a wide variety of problems you'd never have anticipated.

### 5. Don't be intimidated by getting online

The importance of having a clean, clear and engaging website is now essential for any business, and equally important is that the site works on mobile devices too. However, having a great idea and good business savvy doesn't necessarily mean you also have top notch coding or web design skills. Online tools can help make the whole process much easier for those worried about building a decent web presence.

## 6. Delegate, don't micro-manage

Knowing when to hand over the reins is a key business attribute. None of us can do everything all on our own, and it's crucial that we're able to place trust in the people we hire. Micro-managing tasks will end up sucking up all of your time and cause resentment among your team. Instead, learn to delegate those tasks that don't require your personal touch, and give your team the space to succeed on their own terms.

## 7. Reflect your customers' values

Winning and retaining customers is one of the most difficult things to do with a new business, and to do it successfully, they need to personally identify with the business. People want to buy things from a business that reflects their own values, which requires frequent communication about who your company is and what matters to it. It's not just customers, employees also need to buy in to the company's goals and values, so as well as regular external communication don't forget to communicate internally as well.

## 8. Don't go it alone

Building a business is hard work, made much harder if you're doing it all on your own. It's also an important point for start-ups looking to secure funding – investors have learned to focus their investment not on the idea but on the team behind it. It's not ideas that win investment, but teams who inspire confidence that they can deliver on the potential of the idea.

## 9. Establish cash flow

Securing a positive cash flow is essential to any business, but it's a tricky thing to do and tends to hamper early stage businesses in particular. But there are things you can do to help ensure that your business has a steady income stream. One route is by asking clients to pay up front for products and services. Another is to request deposits on work up front and then taking the remaining balance once the work has been delivered.

## 10. Hire great people

When you're starting out, it's crucial that you hire the right people. These aren't necessarily those who have a long list of relevant experiences, but rather those who match your drive and enthusiasm, and would be a good fit for the team. For young businesses, a lack of money and reputation can mean hiring mistakes are costly. Additionally, once you've found the right people, make sure you keep them by empowering them, trusting them to take ownership of their work.

# CHAPTER 7

## CONCLUSION

Beyond giving it your all, it's important to direct your energy to the right tasks – especially at first. Experts say some good first steps in starting a business are researching competitors, assessing the legal aspects of your industry, considering your personal and business finances, getting realistic about the risk involved, understanding timing, and hiring help.